Urban Gleanings

Mark Mahemoff

Urban Gleanings

Acknowledgements

Some of these poems appeared in *Contemporary Australian Poetry*, *Meniscus*, *ACU Poetry Prize Anthology*, *Australian Poetry Anthology*, *The Saturday Age*, *The Best Australian Poems 2013*, *Snorkel*, *POAM Newsletter*, *Cordite Poetry Review*, *Australian Poetry Members Anthology*, *Antipodes*, *Heat* 20, *Small Packages*, *New Shoots Anthology* and *Visible Ink* 23.

Many thanks to Stephen Matthews for his faith in the book and Ken Searle for permission to use his evocative painting as the front cover image.

Many thanks and much gratitude to Robert Gray, Gig Ryan, Paul Kane, Adam Aitken, Peter Bakowski and Kris Hemensley for their valuable friendship and generous support.

This book is dedicated, as always, to Lisa, Abby and Jake.

Urban Gleanings
ISBN 978 1 76041 329 3
Copyright © text Mark Mahemoff 2017
Cover image, *Macdonaldtown Station*, 1999 © Ken Searle,
used with permission

First published 2017 by
GINNINDERRA PRESS
PO Box 3461 Port Adelaide 5015 Australia
www.ginninderrapress.com.au

Contents

Polished	9
Morning triptych	10
Monumental care	11
Rainy twilight, Victoria Park	12
Red and indigo	13
Night Safe Area	14
Childcare centre at night	15
Sight	17
Ignition	18
Double rainbow	19
A new premises	20
A well	21
Samuel Park	22
The myths	23
Mocking time	25
After home time	26
Disabled swing	27
Beside the sleepers	28
Café Clarity	29
Date stamp	30
The 70s	31
Decades	32
My husband	33
Drifting silence	35
Fish in the rain	36
Paving stones	37
Chokos	38
Under the flight path	39
Fullerton and surrounds	40
Gourick Point	41

Her hands	43
Hotel	44
Urban gleanings	45
Loss in three movements	47
Tuckshop revisited	48
Memory Park	49
Stocktaking	50
Parkland	51
Rookwood	53
Neighbourly	54
Her father	55
Butchery	56
King Tide at Twin Waters	57
Weeping tree	58
Scent	59
Setting	60
Summer ice	61
Considerations on QF4O5	62
Mulgrave in spring	63
On leaving and returning	64
Sestoum: a hybrid	65
Storm sticks	66
Renee and Erica	67
Sorry's essence	68
Speaking with tears	71
Glass houses	75
Survey	76
Tense	77
Small plots	78
Yum Cha	79
Kite Surfing, St Kilda	80
For A. at 11	81

Alive and gone   82
Central Station early   84
More lines   85
Flickering light   86
Your return   87

Humbled

It's a dirty business, making love to the world
once we know what it is without
its sweet dresses, decent demeanours, and still
feeling love for it, facing it.

— William Bronk

from *Hotel Lautreamont*

The world, as we know it, sinks into dementia, proving
narrative passé.

— John Ashbery

from *Let's See: Writings on Art from the New Yorker*

If you don't consent to understand a little, on its own terms,
what you dislike, your love loses muscle tone.

— Peter Schjeldahl

From *How to be Perfect, Collected Poems*

Take care of things close to home first. Straighten up your room
before you save the world. Then save the world.

— Ron Padgett

Polished

A homeless man looks up
at trousered legs with polished shoes

and smiles at remembering
being amongst it,

leading the pack,
then trying to keep up.

Now he's a pilot fish
and the city is his shark.

We try to swim past him
but he mocks our every move.

Morning triptych

1.

Clouds are a slow drift of smoke
early one morning in May.
A neon sign glows optimistically
for a handful of yawning commuters.
Its brightness seems unquenchable,
like awareness of desire,
all the more luminescent because it must end.

2.

On the bus a barefoot woman
in filthy clothes is doubled over
like a freeze frame of a diver
in tuck position.
When she raises her head
you can just make out
a green teardrop tattoo
on her left earlobe.

3.

At 6.30 a.m. street lights silently snap off.
The air is frigid.
Grey, boiling movement in the distance
turns out to be pigeons
bullying each other
for their share of thrown crumbs.
The word pizzicato comes to mind,
and the sudden music of their disbanding
when I come too close.

Monumental care

We are pleased to announce,
in addition to general maintenance,
a monument care service.

For a small annual fee,
if you cannot attend
to your loved one's grave,
we will remove leaves, debris,
bird droppings and weeds,
wash it down fortnightly,
and report any damage or decay.

As for your grief
which waxes and wanes;
the guilt and regret
that claws at your dreams;
all the love and hate
that went unexpressed;
that's none of our business:
we wish you all best.

Rainy twilight, Victoria Park

My left hand grips a yellow strap as the bus jerks its bulk through unreasonable traffic. We are exiting the city in a westerly direction, crammed languidly together, halting briefly at Railway Square. A pushy crowd bullies its way aboard while several desperate passengers attempt to alight. The grumpy driver shouts, 'Three more. That's it. I'm not leaving until you move all the way down the back!' Few who are sitting look up to notice an elderly man and pregnant woman. Riskily vertical, they make the best of it. Most of us are trying to be patient. Some conjure images of home: a warm meal, a soft couch, a kiss, an empty room. Others commune with their iPhones while The Mexican Hat Dance and The Odd Couple ringtones randomly erupt. Tolerating this is like passing a test until the reds, greens and blues of neon signs mingle with rain spattered on my window, converting it to an abstract expressionist canvas. We screech to a stop where Chippendale segues into Darlington. Victoria Park looms, eerily unlit. Invisible now is its lily-choked pond complete with pristine chocolate headed ducks and eels which raise their slimy heads in daylight for hot chips and chucked lumps of white bread. It's deserted like a schoolyard at midnight. With a hiss of doors we press on past Sydney University's expanse of hedge and sandstone; past the always exorbitant BP station at the corner of Missenden; past the 24-hour McDonalds; then right into Norton, the CBD far behind us, rendered indistinct by short-sightedness, drizzle and distance.

Red and indigo

The temperature rises
and September starts to sneeze.

A horizon is spray-painted on.
Masking tape's been used
to demarcate ocean from sky.

There is little vegetation
which isn't geometric.
Untamed landscape
is fenced off for protection.

Buildings shoot up
the way trees once did.

As night arrives
cranes become idle.
Their long-necked logos
glow indigo and red.

Night Safe Area

A train has just pulled out.
Rain is dripping from awnings.

There's a man with tattooed calves –
green tracings not filled in –

and a woman with scar-slashed cheeks
explaining timetables
to the nervous person next to her.

It's me and other misfits,
old, young and wrecked,
huddled under shelter,
waiting to be moved.

Childcare centre at night

It's a cold winter evening.
The sandpit's been raked
and awkwardly concealed
with a worn-out tarp.

A battered dump truck's
been zoomed around all day
and carefully parked
near the mini plastic dishwasher.

Someone's old stroller
has been pushed into a corner.
It looks precisely
like an inside-out umbrella.

It's dark outside
but inside a light's still shining.
A worker's there minding
the child who's always picked up last.

The parent, a father, finally arrives
in a jokey jumble of lame excuses
while his child, smiling tearfully,
throws itself into his arms.

The gate is then bolted
and the last sounds heard
are car doors slamming
and ignitions being turned.

An unfamiliar silence
has been locked in for the night.
Is there anything emptier
than an empty childcare centre?

Sight

That woman with grey/blue eyes
must now face old age
which her grey/blue eyes
did not see coming.

Or is it me and my fear
staring back from the bathroom mirror,
wishing my sight was less clear?

Ignition

I turn the ignition switch
while a morning sky quickly takes up light.

An upstairs blind blinks open.
I wave to the drowsy silhouette
and she waves back as I pull out
of the drive way, progress up the street
and notice a church spire, solemn,
against Monday's brightening backdrop.

There's a fuss at someone's front door.
A father is leaving; a toddler is resisting;
a mother is managing her brand-new vocation.

This cast of characters have always been here;
anonymous actors in a long-running play,
randomly recast each day, each year.

Double rainbow

A double rainbow arched over Leichhardt. Old and young alike looked up and smiled. It was the vision they'd been waiting for. Pessimists became optimists and optimists felt vindicated. Crime ceased. Cars slowed down or parked to watch. Everyone knew it would only last as long as rain and sunlight joined forces. Everyone's gaze was held by this vision. The promise of gold that had never been kept. And even as night came, long after it had disappeared, they all held the memory of what had occurred. There were small pools of hope left on every street.

A new premises

I arrive with lunch
to find you clearing out

years of junk and dust.
You say the man next door

has gone bust
and now buys stuff from the tip,

polishes it up
and flogs it off to make ends meet.

I point to what's left of your workshop
crammed with half-useful things

and contemplate how dreams
often end up in mothballs.

We pull down the old roller door
and visit your new premises.

It's still a huge expanse
of empty cubic metres.

Side by side we stand in the middle of nothing.
I'm finally learning how to be a son.

A well

I recall my great-grandparents
like drawing water from a well.
The taste and touch.
The sight and smell.

My grandmother was never
youthful to me.
Nor was my grandfather.
Their childhood was a mystery.

Now it's obvious
I'm heading that way
I look at my own children
and don't know what to say.

I was once like you are now
I think but can't relay.
Sometimes innocence feels close
but mostly far away.

Samuel Park

The home-time bell triggered
an avalanche of bodies,
graffiti scrawled bags snatched,
barging into late afternoon.

Some waited for mothers or buses.
I'd make my way home
through Samuel Park's scrubbiness
with its stainless steel slippery dip
which fried your arse
in the weekend's midday heat.

The bushes were a perfect teenage hideaway—
Tailor-mades, laughter and kisses—
then a shortcut through Glen Avon's driveway
and right to your front door.

On Cracker Night the neighbourhood
flocked to Samuel Park.
Adults grew tipsy
and gazed into the bonfire.
Kids chucked in dud Roman candles
which burst into spasms of colour.

My house near Samuel Park
was razed years ago.
My family dispersed.
My old school shut.
And now I live
many light years from there,
the flare of those memories
all but extinguished.

The myths

In this final photograph
your fading eyes
match the pale blue lounge chair
engulfing your frailty.

It was the final time we met
in your ultimate months
after you relented
and entered the nursing home.

You were born in 1918
in a village so sequestered
that all its inhabitants
flocked to watch a car drive through.

And the temperature would plummet
with such bitterness
that milk was delivered
in a frozen block.

I remember your apartment
in Albury Road
where I slept in darkness
as if wrapped in black velour.

And your homemade biscuits
which I pilfered surreptitiously,
creeping to your pantry
in sleepless early morning.

But you were preoccupied
in ways I couldn't fathom.
Not only with your husband's
gruff infirmity,
but with general discontent
at how life had unfolded.

It was rumoured you were once
a promising pianist
(though I never heard you play a single note).
Some said you had the talent
to have made it a career
if this or that hadn't stymied your progress.

Though now there are great-grandchildren
I'm glad you came to know
who will only remember
the kindness you acquired.

And a kind of accomplishment
when your oldest son, my father,
reached sixty-nine years old
not long before you died.

If only, if only I hear myself say.
But in lieu of recognition
that should have come to you

I hope these words might serve
in some belated way
dear Mary, my grandmother,
dear Manya, my babushka.

Mocking time

You imagine that old man
slumped on a leather lounge
in the posh shopping centre
is dreaming of an old man
he saw years ago
slumped on a park bench.

You're in a slump before work,
knowing that regardless
of how the body looks,
the mind might still be
toned and supple,
playing in the sun
or involved in sexual acts.

A child is staring,
bewildered by my age
and how I arrived here.
Leaping and skipping,
she can't imagine
such a journey,
having already begun it herself
irreversibly.

After home time

Handball and hopscotch grids
are now bereft.
A single street lamp
falters into light,
lending a shadow
to the Moreton Bay Fig tree,
its huge roots breaking through
concrete and bitumen,
toppling a wall
in extreme slow motion.

From a demountable classroom
adjacent to the main hall,
sounds of an evening class:
djembe drumming for beginners.

They return to their cars
sweaty and smiling,
chatting in dribs and drabs.

A weary cleaner
is coiling an extension cord
while your head plays
a song by Cat Stevens.

Disabled swing

At the park's periphery
it waits and rusts.
An ungainly contraption
fenced off from the rest of us.

I've never seen it used, not once.
Today an able-bodied kid sits
where, apparently, a wheelchair fits.
He soon heads for the slippery dips.

It started out as a bright idea
by some well-meaning alderman or mayor.
You picture the inauguration,
the sausage sizzle, the fanfare.

Yesterday the swing was irrelevant.
Tomorrow won't be any different.
It remains what it's always been:
a noble gesture, an indictment,
the room's unmentioned elephant.

Beside the sleepers

Bits of things glinting and rusting: condoms, syringes, bleached chicken bones still nesting in greasy, foil-lined bags. Huge, abandoned coils of cable. A credit card and driver's license, their photographs smiling side by side near the wallet home they once occupied (with eyes squeezed shut you imagine the word stolen shrieked, frantic telephone calls cancelling everything).

Long, unpunctuated summer days under which rails bake and buckle. Ants and their chaotic single-mindedness. Copper-plated skinks scrambling through a crackling of leaves. Crude graffiti sniggering and smirking from concrete pylons. A three-legged blue tongue munching on a frothing snail. Overgrown gully after overgrown gully, each one a tangle of purple or yellow flowered vines. In this context they're weeds, home to half-inflated soccer balls kicked out of sight, cried over and forgotten. Last week's ancient newspapers yellowing.

We jerk to a standstill and halt inexplicably for some minutes in the middle of nowhere, then lurch back into movement, rolling through a landscape of telegraph wires strung tightly across summer.

Café Clarity

Some have come for banter
over Turkish toast and coffee.
Others for respite from traffic
and a kind of public privacy.

You count yourself amongst the latter.
But your lack of sociability
is an annoying barrier
to this waiter's affability

'Give me some space!' you think but can't say
while he continues completely undeterred,
as if it's his decision that you'll both be friends,
regardless of the message your silence sends.

'You've really enjoyed your breakfast, I see!'
he notifies the man at a table near the door
who's desperate to read his newspaper in silence,
who's also annoyed by the sparkling repartee.

Eventually he leaves you to your paper and pen
while making you aware of a deeply ingrained flaw.
An inability to state with directness and transparency
what you don't want, or need less of, or more.

Date stamp

July 1979
stamped on the back
of a photo
of a fourteen-year-old
in a scout uniform.

Three fingers on his right hand
raised,
his pink cheeks unstubbled,
his belt-buckle straining
from a pre-pubescent paunch.

The day is sunny
but his face is dark.
It appears he's seen
far too much for his age.

That boy now a man.
The man still that boy.
There's nothing momentous
in any of this.

In the background, out of focus,
parents chat
over an open car door
as if it's a back fence.

The 70s

1.

Long before an overpass mowed down all those stately terraces, schools offered their grounds to the public during summer holidays. Kiddy art classes with pottery wheels, enamelling, candle making. Mums in brown Maxis dropping their kids off with snack packed plastic boxes. The soundtrack was Elton's 'Crocodile Rock'. Captain and Tennille's 'Love Will Keep Us Together'. This and more schlock blared from 2SM's tinniness. Late in the day Mum picked you up, smelly and exhausted, arms full of clumsy craft, heads packed with moments which have morphed into flashbacks.

2.

Her Belfast accent. Her plain Craven As. Her endless cups of tea. Her sparse grey pubic hair startling each morning. The dinners she concocted which crept wetly to the edges of our plates. And parents' voices crackling from abroad. The baton passed, operator to operator. Desperate from thousands of miles, you clung to their cadences, like ropes thrown overboard in darkness.

3.

Boundaries dissolved as guests grew tipsy around the sparkling pool. Whatever happened to crochet bikinis? When it came time to eat they staggered to the barbecue, glasses of Ben Ean and Mateus Rosé slopping. The first bite was horribly confusing. Mouthfuls puked onto the lawn. Eucalyptus twigs had been used for kindling. All the snags and steaks tasted like cough lollies. Everyone dined out on that story for years.

Decades

Both gone now. Both.
Always that glass of orange juice
covered with a square of cardboard
and three prunes marooned
on the same small dish.

She laid them out each night for him,
ready for the morning.
Teeth gritted.

And for her,
a small shot of brandy after breakfast
to smooth the edges.
It went on like this for decades.

Then overnight the discontent vanished.
Her life was so suddenly lightened by his death,
it took some time to fully register.

My husband

It's not that he's a bad man,
he's just so introverted, baulking
at any social gathering.

He's always in his head
and I'm sick of being in there with him,
amongst those grey, convoluted folds.

It's stifling. I just want to party.
Who knows how much time I've got?
And I want more sex, in different ways.

I'm beyond prudishness.
I'll be frank with you.

There's a guy hanging around,
a work colleague, who I know
wants to fuck me. And I'm afraid I will. I'm afraid.

I know it wouldn't be a long term thing.
Who wants a long-term thing anyway?
That's what I've got with my husband.

He's a good man. My husband not the other guy.
But he finds it hard to get it up.
Or, to be more accurate, keep it up.
Do you mind if I talk like this?

I hate talking like this.
I feel so guilty. But life's short, as I said.
Is it a crime to want to have fun? I feel like a criminal.

And my husband just thinks I'm ridiculous.
When I get annoyed, he asks me which pill I'm on today,
the blue one or the white one. They're for my hormones.

But I don't need to tell you that.
It's so demeaning. It's not about pills, or hormones,
it's about desire. Desire. Desire.

Drifting silence

Spry on a chilled morning,
she asks to go outside,
while he, ten times her age,
starts up like a used car.

She begs him until,
for the sake of some peace,
he tells her to rug up,
they'll go out for a short while.

'Look, Dad,' she shouts,
'balloons, balloons!'
She's right, there they are,
in massive, drifting silence.

And every so often
a brief burst of flame
to keep them airborne
in a soft, grey sky.

Standing, shivering
in a nappy and pyjamas
they watch the flotilla
disappear into their past.

Fish in the rain

Mid November
and the temperature drops.
A sudden downpour
pockmarks the pond.

Weather is moody
and indecisive
think the goldfish
who take cover under duckweed.

This is life scaled down.
A lizard's pulsing dimple heartbeat.
Ants dismantling a cockroach.
Birds rehearsing their sunset repertoire.

Paving stones

The olive tree next door
is gnarled and overgrown.
It dumps its bitter cherries
onto our paving stones.

Beside it there's another tree
I can't identify.
Its blossoms are so purple
they almost make me cry.

Two rainbow lorikeets
are swinging on a branch.
They're feasting on ripe persimmons:
April's sweetest treats.

What's left of this abundance
remains hanging in tatters.
In darkness flying foxes
take care of such matters.

Chokos

Chayote, pimpinela, pipinola, christophine are just a few names given to this cousin of the melon.

A bunch of them appeared at our local farmers' market, like schoolmates you haven't caught up with for decades.

In my formative years they sprawled by the hundreds, tangled amongst passionfruit hanging from our paling fence.

Served boiled, we often had a half each for dinner, a nob of butter melting where the seed had once been.

Whole and hanging from the vine, with a gnarled, softly prickled lime green skin, they looked poisonous,

like those large pods that hang from trees whose broken branches ooze with Selley's wood glue sap.

I remember their bland and innocuous flavour, something we grew accustomed too, familiar and ubiquitous as squabbles between parents.

There were rumours back then that Cherry Ripes were made from chokos. That food dye and flavouring were added, then the bar-shaped mixture dipped into chocolate.

Strange to think that now I'd pay dearly for a choko when for so long they were plentiful and free for the picking.

Under the flight path

It commenced with milling and chat, grief hidden and dispersed
among abandoned buildings which once housed
madness and those who sometimes fail to cope.

The small, broken crowd soon gathered and sat on prefab plastic seats
positioned under a huge, old tree whose still, long life
has watched every living creature vanish.

And like a Quaker meeting, there was speechlessness
interspersed with statements, anecdotes,
and readings of his poems.

And because we were under the flight path each flight of words was cropped
by aviation noise, the way a sulphur crested cockatoo
will naturally and rudely interrupt a conversation.

We were all somehow helpless but helped by sharing this experience,
though also sad at knowing each of us would get our turn
sooner than we'd like to think.

And then, with what felt to me like brutal suddenness,
a recording of his voice was broadcast,
its northern English cadences softened by exile.

And my eyes began to moisten, not just because I'd miss him,
but with the pure overwhelm of death's conundrum:
its magnitude and masterful decisiveness.

Fullerton and surrounds

Not far past Crookwell –
where time melds with trees and silence –
the city is a stain
slowly bleached from your thoughts.

Our car dissolves into air.
Only wind resistance
reminds us it exists.

Pausing for a copy
of the *Sydney Morning Herald*,
the engine shudders
and jolts to a halt.

Approaching scrub,
tar crumbles towards dirt
the way a fuse burns to ash.

Later that evening, after alcoholic chat,
we wish each other a goodnight
underneath a sky glutted with stars.

Gourick Point

Tranquil.
A breeze and a beach.
A jetty where tourists dangle lines
at the wrong time of day.

*

Two square blocks of building
with a chimney next to each.
She said, 'It's a coal fired
power station, it's how we
make our money around here,'
and handed him the bait.

*

The day's thermostat has
gone on the blink.
Hot one minute,
chilled the next.
People from the city
dream timeshare
and retirement.
When the holiday ends,
it's back to business.

*

The heat at midday's no joke.
Even kookaburras find it difficult to laugh.
Cicadas seem to be taking your pulse.
Clouds are curds
suspended in a whey sky.

Her hands

Disease spent nine years
pilfering her competence

but her rage still had the power
to leap tall buildings.

With nothing to be done
he stayed while she napped,

then snapped her hands
with his mobile phone.

At the end they were still plump
and free of liver spots.

He kept that image
and examines it at times,

remembers the helplessness,
tears up, then moves on.

Hotel

In the swish hotel lobby
flight attendants do a kind of happy dance.

Freshly showered and shaved,
they are ready for the airport bus.

Then it's up, up and away:
Champagne, smoked salmon

and stroking for first class,
a smirk and pretzels for economy.

Outside, life bats the double glazing
like a slow blowfly.

Near the gleaming brass revolving door
a man and his dog are camped.

There's water in a stainless steel bowl,
a corrugated placard describing hard luck,

and an upturned hat with a smattering of coins.
Next to him a cleaner polishes his pane.

Urban gleanings

1/

Bitumen shadowed and sunlight squinting
from gloss tiles at the awning flap.
A bush pruned flat
as a West Point haircut.

2/

Jostling. A yellow line
between staying and going.

3/

A woman smiles
and smooths her black skirt.
Another has long hair
held in a sloppy bun.
Intimate strands
wisp around her ears.

4/

Each platform is a short story
skimmed in an effort
to finish the anthology.

5/

An escalator challenges you
to stand still
or move on steps
which are themselves moving.

6/

The crane far above
is a giant skeleton
a museum relic
whose flesh is absent.
How did this animal
once look?

7/

A cockatoo pristine
as a newly drafted blueprint
perched on the cliff edge
of a half-demolished building.

8/

Through a night of hard rain
your bedroom is an air raid shelter.
Sudden daylight is a shopfront window
squeegeed clean.

9/

You awake
to switch off the bathroom light
but it's a full moon
beaming through the window.

Loss in three movements

1/

Trauma connects both of you.
If that was resolved,
what would be left?

They both laughed hard at this,
then she resumed her sobbing.

Why did you attend?
Because she asked me too.

2/

Six years since her last breath
and not a week goes by
when they don't feel disbelief.
Life's become more serious
because of this.

3/

He was born at the inception of flight
and died with a plasma TV left on.
His era witnessed continents of people disappear.
Regimes topple and rise.

Tuckshop revisited

Transport me back to play lunch
for that lost opportunity,

let it be rewritten,
her warm hand in mine,

not withdrawn but held,
my voice not quivering,

my arm around her waist,
fearless and natural,

both of us standing
on frigid asphalt,

our urgent eyes
locked in adolescent ardour,

every teacher and student
in the school ground

watching with envy:
utterly spellbound.

Memory Park

At Memory Park it's always autumn.
Children swing like pendulums.
Arrogant magpies forage
and stare into the distance.
Boys wear superhero capes.
Spiders spin their silky geometries.

At Memory Park
there are wood and concrete benches.
Graffiti is as strange as fear.
The young don't age.
The old don't die.

At Memory Park
grazed knees heal instantly.
Bread is used to swab
the few tears that are shed.
Then it's broken and shared
with anyone who's hungry.

Stocktaking

'After 26 years of owning this bookshop we regret to inform you that Mr M has passed. They tell me it was peaceful. I'm not sure what that means. Be that as it may, I'd like everyone to know that from now on he will be a palpable absence. You'll think you hear him rearranging shelves. You'll sense him leafing through recent arrivals or dusting unloved hardbacks in the bargain bin. You'll imagine you see him greeting customers. This is only your shock and bewilderment, your wish that he'd never departed.

I was told there is no need for tears. After all, isn't he in a better place? While this belief is a comfort to some, it does not console his wife who he once described as his first and last love. They were planning to retire and couldn't wait to enjoy the cash they'd salted away through all those decades of dedicated work. This isn't how it was meant to be.

She imagined cruises and drinks by the pool. Time spent with grandchildren correcting the mistakes they'd made as parents. The two of them talking for hours and suddenly looking up to wonder where the time had gone. Now her future looms as an empty, hostile place.

But it can truthfully be said Mr M prized his work. It was his vocation. He called this bookshop his "second home".

And in that final snapshot he's smiling, not knowing like all of us when the end will come. They've displayed this image on the front counter like a mantelpiece.'

Parkland

On a steep hill
I grip the handbrake nervously.
There are four of us. Two under ten.
The day is airbrushed grey.
We slam our doors and head to a café.
The children are rubbery on their legs.
Both of us have seasoned into adulthood.

The Sunday brunch crowd disperses
as we commandeer a table.
Heartburn looms in the distance.
You stare at me. I look away.
I stare at you. You look away.
We both stare at these kids
who don't belong to us:
their charming and irritating pinkness.
Not a blemish between them.
I stroke my face and feel
the greying weekend stubble.

We set off for the park of my childhood.
Ferns, moss, creeks, waterfalls, swings,
slippery dip, see-saw, tennis courts,
cricket pitches, kiosk and public toilets.
Families and their fragments.
Children and dogs
as if these words are inseparable.

It's been more than twenty years
since coming with my family
to let our collie wade chest-deep
amongst tadpoles and mud.
The frogs are now almost extinct.
The collie long gone.
Only tins and bottles flourish.

We climb steps that lead to dirt tracks
which lead to even more steps.
We hold hands too tightly and then let go.
Large and small fingers moistly intertwined.
Painted wooden signs show us the way.

Rookwood

Since your disappearance
I've stewed in insomnious darkness,
waiting for a sign of the hereafter.

Your life was full of sound and fury
signifying something
I still don't understand.

Your absence has been bursting
with the noise of grandchildren
and the living world still turning.

You've become one more meal
for worms and history.
The sound of your voice
is now static in my memory.

Your self-designed tombstone –
the talk of the necropolis –
stays largely unvisited
amongst hectares of loss.

Neighbourly

Walking at night towards home,
you see them looming
from the opposite direction.

Her smile is a flashlight.
It illuminates a dog and husband
who bounds up to introduce himself,
as if marking his territory.

You greet the three of them
and go on your way,
her smile secreted
like a sin among your thoughts.

Her father

Remember when we gathered at that harbour inlet
when your father was reduced to a canister of ashes?

We ventured onto rocks until it seemed safe to cast them,
like so much burley, into turbulent water.

A rude gust crudely blew some back
onto dry-cleaned pants and polished shoes.

Those of us who weren't immediately involved
stood back and waited until the wavelets dispersed him.

Then all of us picnicked on a grassy embankment.
We laughed and cried and said nothing about Death.

Butchery

How can you smile
with death daily
at your fingertips?

You take the flesh I've purchased
and kindly slice it into cubes.
I watch unmoved
and peruse the carnage
ordered neatly behind glass.

The oldest butcher is the happiest of all.
His face a ruddy record
of all the beer he's sunk.

At closing time he scrubs
and polishes the surfaces,
never quite erasing
another day's crimes.

King Tide at Twin Waters

All night squalls turn towels to flags.
Cicadas harmonise with surf
that laps at searing bitumen.

A mesh of vegetation reinforces dunes
which one can perch on
in January's kiln heat.

Each news flash blares, 'King tides are here!'
One is well advised to keep one's distance
and be rapt.

You do and are,
watching the ocean tear at the shore:
prey and predator.

Weeping tree

The suburb had collapsed into sleep
when screech of speed
and crunch of metal
tore us out of shallow dreams.

Some raised their blinds
to see what must have been a car,
exhaust fumes billowing,
the motor revving dangerously,
as if the driver, despite his death,
was anxiously attempting to exit the scene.

Tow trucks formed a pack,
tactless as vultures,
while babies in flats
wailed their limited vocabulary.

Within hours it took shape:
scrawled notes and flowers
taped to a tree.

And every year since
they gather and weep
for the sixteen-year-old boy
disqualified from adulthood.

Scent

At the corner of Eric and Balmain,
at Spring's unveiling,
jasmine ignores traffic,
shamelessly secreting a tropical scent.

When I lift you to inhale its headiness –
because words are no replacement
for experience –
a kookaburra raucously
announces itself.

       Bulldozers, earth movers
and dump trucks encircle us.
The slushy ground's become
a minefield of puddles.

Words must not be
a replacement for experience.
This is how we tessellate
throughout each other's days.

Setting

Sunset filtered through an olive tree
and a melon rind moon.
Tomorrow, to entice lorikeets,
you'll mix warm water, bread and honey.
They'll come and feast in a flurry of colours,
fooled into thinking the concoction is nectar.

It's cool now amongst the distant scraping
of knives and forks on crockery
and birds which begin and end each day with chatter.
Clouds are golden lint
clinging to the sky's blue fabric.
A copper-coloured skink
is a thought vanishing.

Be in this time now wholly
and be calm, calmed.
There is nothing more or less
than this.

Summer ice

It's thought to have been there
for sixteen million years
but who knows now,
maybe twenty, maybe ten more.

You imagine polar bears,
so white and savage,
clinging to their icy rafts.

This long ride seems to be ending.
Luxurious for some,
wretched for most.

Finally we're all reduced
to passengers in steerage
on this titanic earth
gradually sinking.

Considerations on QF4O5

While his family dreamed deeply,
the father would leave each morning,
feeling through dark silence
for car keys
         and come home at 6 p.m.,
half an hour before dinner,
fall into a chair, shield himself
with a force-field of exhaustion.
         The pre-pubescent son
danced manically around
to make the father laugh,
honing his clowning skills
while burying pain
like all good jesters.
         The teenage daughter was nowhere to be seen.
She may have been in her bedroom studying
or being felt up by a boy
soothing her aching heart.
         And in the background
always the mother's toxic eyes
radiating discontent.
         This nuclear family,
each member a fragment of shrapnel,
speeding away from one another
towards an imagined better future.
Even now the dust
is settling.

Mulgrave in spring

Before her plain, pine box
was lowered into darkness
the minister called a halt to the service.

'The reason I've requested this hiatus
is to highlight the offensiveness
of rushing someone to their grave.'

'You must stop for a moment and think about your life,
then think about the impact made
by those no longer with us.'

'And finally consider your own disappearance.
The effect it will have
on those who remain.'

Shovels were then plunged into cold, wet clay
and the pit was slowly filled.
There is nothing left to say.

On leaving and returning

It seems these days
he takes more of himself away
when he leaves
and goes out into the cold.

He leaves them behind in the warmth
and tries to hold onto some of it
while he's gone.

It seems these days
they let him go more easily. If he's lucky
on returning he's greeted with a kiss
and a small, soft body,

or is welcomed by them
going about their business,
not doubting that he's back
and solidly there to stay.

There is this need to feel useful,
to be held in their mind,
to be held.

Increasingly, he holds himself,
knowing he's all he has, ultimately,
knowing they're important
but still visitors in his life.

Sestoum: a hybrid

How will I cope with the absence of this vista?
My arms encircle you, absorbing your acceptance.

Applying logic to chaos, we call it the next phase
while dreading how the past might spill into our future.

My arms encircle you, absorbing your future.
Outside cars, like birds, augment the vista.

While dreading how the past might spill into our phase
we fill our flimsy boxes and move to the next acceptance.

Outside cars, like birds, augment the phase.
There is evidence to show that we face a shocking future.

We fill our flimsy boxes and move to the next vista.
There's no way of knowing the shape of our acceptance.

There is evidence to show that we face a shocking acceptance.
While everyone makes plans for an invisible phase

there is no way of knowing the shape of our future.
We must understand that the past was once our vista.

How will I cope with acceptance: the absence of this vista?
Applying logic to future chaos, we call it the next phase.

Storm sticks

He balanced his ciggies
on the edges of things,
letting ash droop
to the point of almost breaking.

He baked bread for a living
and spent his spare time cleaning
to earn extra cash
for scratchies and beer.

'I've been overseas just once!'
he'd proudly announce
and often sounded racist
but was always kind to strangers.

A confirmed bachelor,
he never seemed lonely.
And after he died
from a cough he'd ignored

I remembered
that he called umbrellas storm sticks
and laughed at having known him
and cried at having lost him.

Renee and Erica

Basel, 1940.
Two three-year-old girls
cocooned in thick coats
are standing in a laneway
clutching gloved hands.

In the dull background
giant adults mill.
A woman, half-obscured by an iron gate,
is watching the photo being composed.

Right now it's safe
in their gaol of neutrality.
Beyond the perimeter
Europe gargles blood.

Sorry's essence*

I move today we honour, we reflect
on mistreatment of the oldest history, indigenous people
who were stolen, blemished in our nation
the time has now come to turn Australia's history
by righting the future
we apologise for profound grief and suffering and loss
and pain and indignity and degradation and sheer brutality and hurt
of mothers and fathers and brothers
and sisters and families and communities
breaking up inflicted on a proud people and the spirit
healing, heart, embraces
never, never again
solutions, respect, resolve, responsibility
origins are truly equal
remove a great stain
do so early
an elegant, eloquent and wonderful woman
has travelled a long way to be with us
she remembers the love and the warmth
and the kinship of those days
she remembers she insisted on dancing
rather than just sitting and watching
she remembers the coming of the welfare men
tears flowing, clinging
complex questions
it was as crude as that
Tennant Creek and Goulburn Island
and Croker Island and Darwin and Torres Strait

She was 16
a broken woman fretting
ripped away from her
it's a good thing that you are surrounded by love
Sorry
And remarkably, extraordinarily, she had forgiven him
there is something terribly primal about these
a deep assault
stony, stubborn and deafening
leave it languishing
human decency, universal human decency
deliberate, calculated, explicit, and notorious
Generally by the fifth and invariably by the sixth generation
all native characteristics are eradicated
they are profoundly disturbing, well-motivated, justified
an apology well within the adult memory span
a point in remote antiquity
it is well within the adult memory span of many of us
therefore we must also be the bearer of their burdens as well
the darkest chapters
with the facts, the evidence and the often rancorous public
we are also wrestling with our own soul
cold, confronting, uncomfortable
there will always be a shadow hanging over us
I am sorry
I am sorry
I am sorry
without qualification

Yuendumu, Yabara, Pitjantjatjara
there is nothing I can say today
I cannot undo that
grief is a very personal thing
imagine the crippling effect
it is little more than a clanging gong
a thinly veiled contempt
the gap will set concrete
the truth is a business
halve the appalling gap
back the obscenity
beyond our infantile bickering
Dreamtime

* This poem is constructed entirely from words and phrases taken from Kevin Rudd's 'Sorry' speech as published in *The Sydney Morning Herald* (online version) 13 February 2008.

Speaking with tears*

I received your letter when I was very happy and cheerful.
Anyway, it is enough for me that they are healthy and live.
You want to know about my family it's very sad story.
What a big joke with humanity and human rights.
What we'll remember is how they treat us.

    As the helicopters were flying over our heads
I was crying and my mother was trying to keep me quiet.
I hope one day I can be free but I think only in my dream.
People are dead like chickens. All of us we are crying inside.

    Our life slowly became normal again and it seemed good.
I left my country because of gorilla. Ethnic cleansing was pursued.
And the people who live there were all farmers.
Their dignity, their property, even their virgin daughters are not safe.
I saw their cruelty. I cannot describe it.
And in a way I was treacherous to myself, my family, my people
and to all humen world wide.
You want me to go back? Where?
To where crime is law and law is crime?
My family is still there and I've lost some of them in infinite violence.

    This is some of my story. As you ask.

Finally the so called tax collector team came to our village.
After beating me to death they put me in prison.
How did I travel here?

    Then we saw more officers, razor wire, red soil.
For the second attempt we left in the month of February.
En route the rain started to fall with storms
and the wind went on through the night until morning,
but we were saved (this time we had a good captain);
in the morning he started to fish, he caught some tuna.

When it became light then we found out that
we were on a small, old boat. Days were hot and nights were cold.
We even saw dolphins during the way. They jumped out of the water.
We saw death with our eyes.

There was an old man sitting calmly in the corner and staring
at some point on the boat. A child took the old man's water bottle
and in a confused state the old man took it back. But then he hugged the child
and held the water bottle to the mouth of the child. The engine sound was now
like the best music.

Sunsets and sunrises help you ponder what life has in store for you.
The present overtakes the past and sadness overtakes the future.
Patience would be a virtue, but the truth lies in the period of torture.

Imagine my friend that I am still wearing the same clothes
that I came in with two years ago. I think the world has forgotten me.
I am talking about a true prison, where thoughts are killed
and death is always knocking at the door.

Also there are pigeons and they raise their babies here.
The only thing we can do is watch their freedom.
In here we really need your prayer.

You probably just watched and read about what happened here,
but the fact is bigger than that. They entered the compound with the blue unif
so that you couldn't see any part of their bodies. They were like an army.

Some people smoke like me and other people
want to smoke in their bed. We have anti standard life here.

Dear unknown friend. Here is always dark and foggy.
We can not see some metres away and everything is fence, fence, fence.
Do not have hope that I am well. When I went for surgery I had to go in hand

Every day afternoon they take my family to walk near the river.
They have a beautiful dog, he is tame and play with my children .
Kookaburra! Oh yes, I almost can see it everyday.

Through the years I have nothing but supplications and tears, t unfortunately the tears have ceased and I am left with nothing t the supplications.

You have got a lot of fun but we do not have any.
ır fun is watching the fences. We have some shelf books but all of them
: very old and expire. We have one doctor twice per week but my information
better than his. We call him doctor Panadol.

Every morning, when I open my eyes I see four lines of fence around
d I must say good morning to them. When you become afflicted
u can speak with your mother or your friends. But Sometimes I speak
my mother's photo.

Once a month I sit and wait for the moon.

 the morning you wake up his songs. Also at night you sleep in his songs. What
) you think about a little bird? Please mum don't leave a little bird alone.

ıe smooth breeze blows continuously from the sunrise side.

nust live in here, I don't want to live in here. I myself am passing
e worst moments of my life. It is nearly one year that I am in this unending journey.
ur hair is getting white and our teeth are getting black.
ıank you so much for the chamomile tea.
eel like I'm in a grave with four walls.
eel like a defenceless bird that escapes from the claws of the dreadful vultures,
ıly to land in the hands of the ruthless hunter.
put my fingers crossed for you.
elieve me, between us there is no one who is criminal.
don't know what to do.
ront of me mountain and behind me tiger.
hey are trying to kill us slow slow.

Our morning starts with fear, the day is spent in limbo and evening ends in def
I am here alone, I send love for your dog and cats.

> We spoke together with our tears.
> The hometown of humanity is only in the heart.
> But I now find in this world
> everywhere the sky has the same colour.

* This poem is constructed entirely from parts of letters contained in *From Nothing to Zero: Letters from Refugees in Australia's Detention Centres*, edited by Meaghan Amor ar Janet Austin (Lonely Planet, 2003). Original grammatical and syntactical errors have been left uncorrected.

Glass houses

Lucky to be here enclosed in glass
at the corner of Park and Elizabeth
all routes have changed
a different view is forced
dig in and rebel
Russia launches missiles
Syria is a basket case
up to its armpits
in tears and blood
you safely make pronouncements
on quotas and queue jumpers
straight lines don't exist
just people
one by one
waves of splinters
corpses washed to shore
all in the same boat

Survey

Things stop getting mentioned.
No one believes this can happen to them.
Imagine being turned

back into a caterpillar
still holding the memory
of having been a butterfly.

Memory is the problem to endure.
If only each day could start out new
with all that's bracing about newness.

Keep working. Keep working.
There's no end to it.
Survey the darkness while recollecting light.

Tense

It's summer but we're wearing winter coats.
Seasons no longer exist,
just moments that evoke them.

On Facebook you have instant access to your past.
People who know people who know people
you once knew.
You see their faces on screen,
faces you haven't seen for years.
You wallow in moments of nostalgia
and move on.
So much information. So much obfuscation.

Rain is falling and the sound it makes
is the sound it's always made.
But this sameness is deceptive,
like the sky's falsely reassuring blueness.
What continues coming but never arrives?
Answer: tomorrow (or so the punch line goes.)
It's funny but no joke.
We're sinking by increments.

Walking in a downpour without an umbrella
creates a bracing vulnerability.
The snails are out in force
in groupings I'd like just this once to call herds.
They remind you of something old and essential.
You take great care to sidestep their slow progress.

Small plots

1/

Fog-bound morning.
Yellow-lidded wheelie bins
litter footpaths
as if dropped
overnight
from the sky.
You negotiate an obstacle course
unable to see the end of the road.

2/

A small plot of lawn
watched over by a gum tree.
Two magpies turn up.
Their songs add notes
to summer's dry soundtrack.

3/

Two men sit outside
on a teak bench
leached to grey.
A tricycle's nearby.
Its blue seat
is faded,
motionless.

They talk
how men often do:
a few words hedging
a plot of silence.

Yum Cha

Elegance and crudeness
are held in perfect balance.

Chopsticks mishandled
spill a dumpling's messy guts.

Straight black hair is swept
into calligraphic ponytails.

Flecks of shallot
coat a little girl's front tooth.

Tiny trees of broccoli
are pruned and piled perfectly.

Chickens feet are severed
just above the ankles.

It's all delivered with a smile
on stainless steel trolleys

in a racket of enjoyment
and unquenchable hunger.

Kite Surfing, St Kilda

A haughty Vizsla sprints for the thrown ball,
almost skids past itself
and forgets to retrieve it.

Its owner sips a glass of red with friends.
A flat green bike path
extends far into the distance.

Dusk. At the end of a long pier
it begins to get cold.
A shivering crowd collects to witness penguins.

Volunteers are there to inform and protect.
'No flashes!' she warns good-naturedly
and distributes squares of red cellophane
to filter harsh torch light.

There's a surfeit of goodwill
and generosity of spirit.
No one meaning anything
or anybody harm.

Meanwhile, a lone kite-surfer
skims night-blackened ocean,
then packs up all his gear
and heads towards home.

For A. at 11

On a ferry
pulling away from shore
sitting near yet distant
she is not your property

yet of you
of her mother
there was a plan
but no idea

and from that she emerged
is emerging
a battered bangle you found
buried in beach sand

is now on her wrist
you battle mawkishness
fully feeling your lack
in her presence

Alive and gone

1/

I left early as usual
and noticed a crow,
black on black,
in the street.

Lidless,
it scanned the terrain
and returned to bothering
what appeared to be
a grey rag
crumpled at its feet.

I stood close enough
to study but not scare it.
The thick, twitching cord
turned out to be a tail.

I abandoned the crow and rat
to their fate
and trapped in my own,
went on my way.

2/

Alive and gone.
A magpie swoops
to tear bread from your hand.

Fish are snatched
by hungry raptors.

Always swimming,
they knew little to begin with,
then that shocking ascension
up towards clouds
and later eaten.

Central Station early

This is pure city.
Tiled stairs and platforms.
Three blokes laughing,
dying for a smoke,
on their way to fishing somewhere
with rods and tackle boxes.

There's industrial detritus on all sides.
Fat timber beams, higgledy-piggledy
next to tracks.
PVC pipe offcuts
and areas in mid-construction
clumsily sequestered
with barricade tape.
A sedentary man with a whistle
who looks like he's never done
anything else.

It's 8 degrees but wind makes it 5.
My train, long gone, is on its way
to Pymble via Gordon
and the air is so perfectly crisp,
the landscape so devoid of foliage,
my mind is filled with trees.

More lines

There's a full fat morning moon
over the inner west.
June is cold, the way it should be.

You recall bumping into X recently.
It had been 10 years.
He was more lined of course,
but his hair had stayed long and thick,
without a strand of grey.

He never grew up.
With any luck
he never will.
A girl half his age
is hanging from his arm
and lapping up his tripe.

He's mastered the art
of wearing life lightly.
You wear it like a hair shirt
ignored on occasion
while looking at the moon.

Flickering light

Allow a dream to stay.
It's just hope, a flickering light
to hold unsnuffed.
Move on
to all the practicalities.

Stay.
A dream allows you
to steer broken paths.
There are cracks
and through them
shoots sprout unchecked.

Sprout hope,
flickering and light.
Gather all the practicalities
and make them your path.
Move on.

Your return

Sunday afternoon.
The sound of birds
surpasses traffic noise.

This room is an island
located off the coast
of obligation.

I hear voices
from the mainland
calling me back.

Waves of ambivalence
slow my return.

www.ingramcontent.com/pod-product-compliance
Lightning Source LLC
Chambersburg PA
CBHW070049120526
44589CB00034B/1678